PROTOZOA

by
Joanna Brundle

Published in 2020 by KidHaven Publishing, an Imprint of Greenhaven Publishing, LLC
353 3rd Avenue, Suite 255, New York, NY 10010

© 2020 Booklife Publishing

This edition is published by arrangement with Booklife Publishing.

Written by: Joanna Brundle
Edited by: Emilie Dufresne
Designed by: Gareth Liddington

Names: Brundle, Joanna.
Title: Protozoa / Joanna Brundle.
Description: New York : KidHaven Publishing, 2020. | Series: Animal classification | Includes glossary and index.
Identifiers: ISBN 9781534530539 (pbk.) | ISBN 9781534530317 (library bound) | ISBN 9781534531499 (6 pack)
| ISBN 9781534530478 (ebook)
Subjects: LCSH: Protozoa--Juvenile literature.
Classification: LCC QL366.B78 2020 | DDC 579--dc23

PHOTO CREDITS

Front Cover – photowind. 2 & throughout – Rattiya Thongdumhyu. 4 – TravelMediaProductions, Kateryna Kon. 6 – Kateryna
Kon. 7 – 3d_man, Lukiyanova Natalia frenta. 8 – Rattiya Thongdumhyu, 3d_man. 9 – Rattiya Thongdumhyu. 10–11– Timonina,
royaltystockphoto.com. 12 – Jubal Harshaw. 13 – Kateryna Kon, Blossom Tomorrow. 14 – 3d_man. 15 – Kateryna Kon, NaniP. 16 –
Choksawatdikorn. 17 – Mr.Parichat chaikuad, Kateryna Kon. 18 – Rattiya Thongdumhyu. 19 – Kateryna Kon, attiya Thongdumhyu.
20–21 – Aldona Griskeviciene. 22 – Lukiyanova Natalia frenta, Aldona Griskeviciene, Kateryna Kon. 23 – Kateryna Kon. 24 – N-2-s.
25 – Kateryna Kon, Jaco Visser. 26 – Christoph Burgstedt, Kletr. 27 – solar22, punghi. 28 – Kateryna Kon, Rattiya Thongdumhyu,
Allexxandar, tarasof, Chatuphon Neelasri, Blacqbook, Ulrike Jordan, Miles Away Photography. 29 – VLADJ55, Rich Carey.

Images are courtesy of Shutterstock.com, unless stated otherwise. With thanks to Getty Images, Thinkstock Photo and iStockphoto.

Printed in the United States of America

CPSIA compliance information: Batch #BS19KL: For further information contact Greenhaven Publishing LLC, New York, New York at
1-844-317-7404.

CONTENTS

Several words in this book have separate singular and **plural** versions. Use this table to help you as you read.

flagellum **flagella**

nucleus **nuclei**

protozoan **protozoa**

pseudopod **pseudopodia**

Words that look like <u>this</u> are explained in the glossary on page 31.

THE ANIMAL KINGDOM

The animal kingdom is estimated to include over eight million known living <u>species</u>. They come in many different shapes and sizes, they each do weird and wonderful things, and they live in every corner of our planet. From the freezing waters of the Arctic to the hottest deserts in the world, animals have <u>adapted</u> to diverse and often extreme conditions on Earth. Although every species of animal is <u>unique</u>, they share certain characteristics with each other. These shared characteristics are used to classify – or group – animals.

The science of classifying different organisms is called taxonomy.

Animals are divided into vertebrates (animals that have a backbone) and invertebrates (animals that do not have a backbone). Vertebrates include mammals, reptiles, amphibians, fish, and birds. Invertebrates include insects and <u>crustaceans</u>. Protozoa are invertebrates that display many animal-like behaviors, such as movement, but they belong to a separate kingdom called Protista. Within the protozoa <u>phylum</u> are smaller groups called subphyla. Protozoa are divided into different subphyla, mainly according to how they move (see page 12 for more information).

Vorticella are protozoa that live in the sea.

(see page 12 for more information).

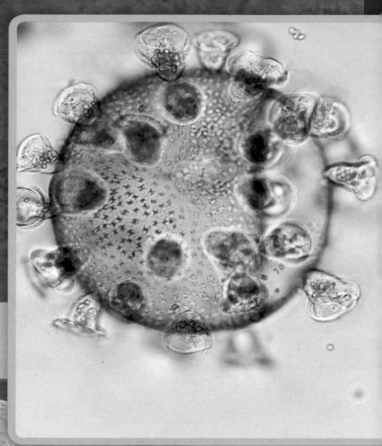

It is estimated that **over 90%** of animals are **invertebrates.**

The name "protozoa" comes from two Greek words, "protos" meaning first and "zoa" meaning animals.

PROTOZOA

Cells are the smallest units of life. They are the building blocks from which all known organisms are made.

Our bodies are made up of trillions of cells, but protozoa are single-celled organisms. This single cell, however, performs all the important processes of life, such as feeding and reproduction. Protozoa are described as eukaryotes (say: you-carry-oats). This word means organisms whose cells have a nucleus. The nucleus acts like a brain, controlling everything the cell does. Most protozoa are heterotrophs (say: het-ur-o-troffs). This word means that they cannot make their own food and have to feed on other organisms.

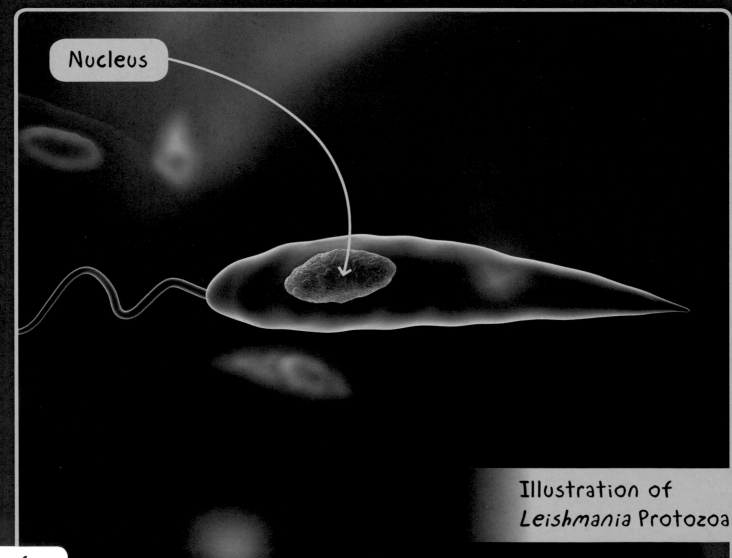

Nucleus

Illustration of *Leishmania* Protozoa

Protozoa have been around for a long time – 1.5 billion years. Estimates of the number of species alive today vary, but there may be as many as 50,000. Fossil records exist for another 34,000 species. Most protozoa are invisible to the naked eye and we have to use a <u>microscope</u> to see them. Many measure less than 0.0002 inch (0.005 mm), but some freshwater species can be up to 0.12 inch (3 mm) long. Most protozoa are able to move around by themselves. Protozoa vary in shape, from the amoeba, which can change shape, to the paramecium, which has a fixed shape.

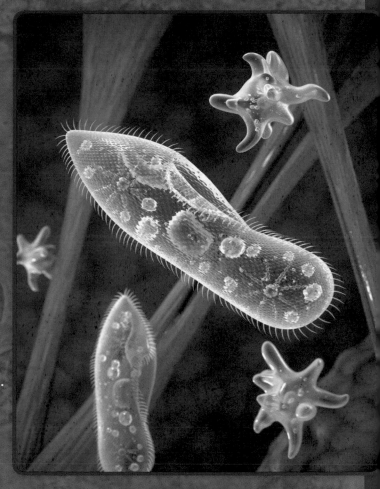

Shape-Changing Amoeba

PROTOZOA CHECKLIST

- 🐾 Single-celled
- 🐾 Heterotrophs (feed on other organisms)
- 🐾 Eukaryotes (cell has a nucleus)
- 🐾 Animal-like behaviors
- 🐾 Mostly motile (able to move)

BODY PARTS

All protozoa have a nucleus (see page 6). Some have two nuclei: a macronucleus (a big brain) and a micronucleus (a small brain). The nucleus of the cell is surrounded by a fluid-like substance called cytoplasm (say: site-o-plaz-um). The outer layer is called ectoplasm and is <u>transparent</u>. The inner layer is called endoplasm. It contains the organelles. Organelles are special structures inside a cell that carry out particular jobs. The cell is contained inside a layer called the membrane.

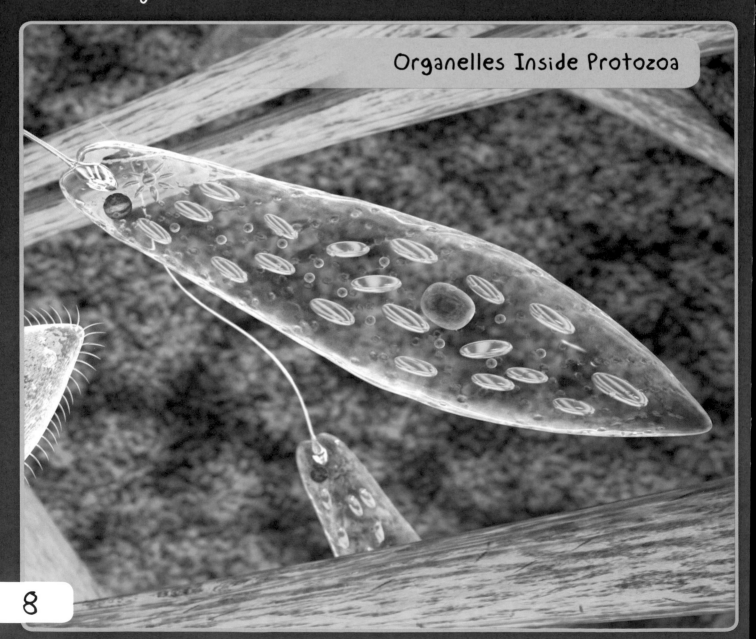

Organelles Inside Protozoa

Some protozoa feed by absorbing food through their cell membranes. Some surround and smother their food using special structures called pseudopodia (say: soo-duh-poh-dee-ah). See page 12 for more information about pseudopodia. Others sweep food particles into the cell through a feeding groove called a cytostome. They do this by wafting hair-like structures called cilia (see page 12). The cytostome is rather like a mouth. All protozoa digest their food in vacuoles, which are stomach-like containers inside the cell.

A View of an Amoeba Through a Microscope

The amoeba is an example of a protozoan that feeds using pseudopodia.

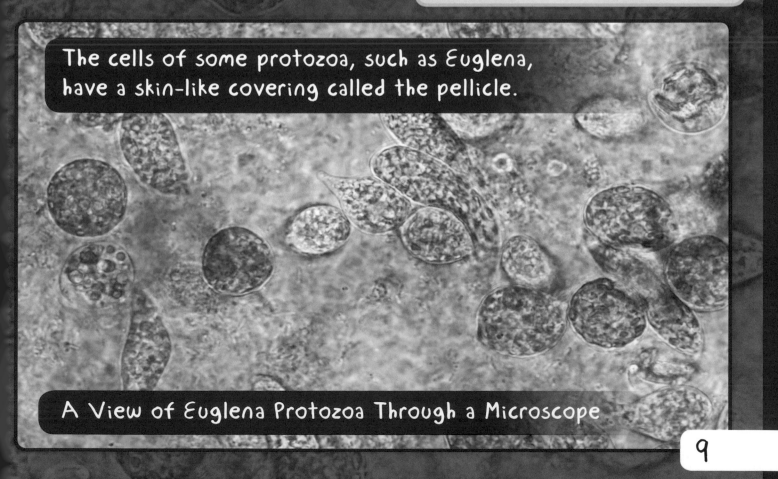

The cells of some protozoa, such as Euglena, have a skin-like covering called the pellicle.

A View of Euglena Protozoa Through a Microscope

Many protozoa, especially freshwater species, have a special vacuole called the contractile vacuole. A protozoan cell absorbs water from its environment. If too much water is taken in, the cell could swell up and burst. The job of the contractile vacuole is to stop this from happening. It does this by gathering water in the cell and then squeezing out the extra water by contracting (making itself smaller). It's like squashing a full bottle of water!

BODY PARTS OF AN AMOEBA

Cytoplasm

Contractile Vacuole

Plasma Membrane

Food Vacuoles

Respiration is a process that takes place in living organisms. Breathing is how humans respire. It allows organisms to make energy from their food but requires <u>oxygen</u> to be taken in and waste products (water and <u>carbon dioxide</u>) to be given out. In most protozoa, this happens through the cell membrane, in a process called diffusion. If there are more oxygen <u>molecules</u> in the water on the outside of the cell than on the inside, then oxygen molecules can pass through the cell membrane into the cell to even things out. Carbon dioxide passes out in the same way.

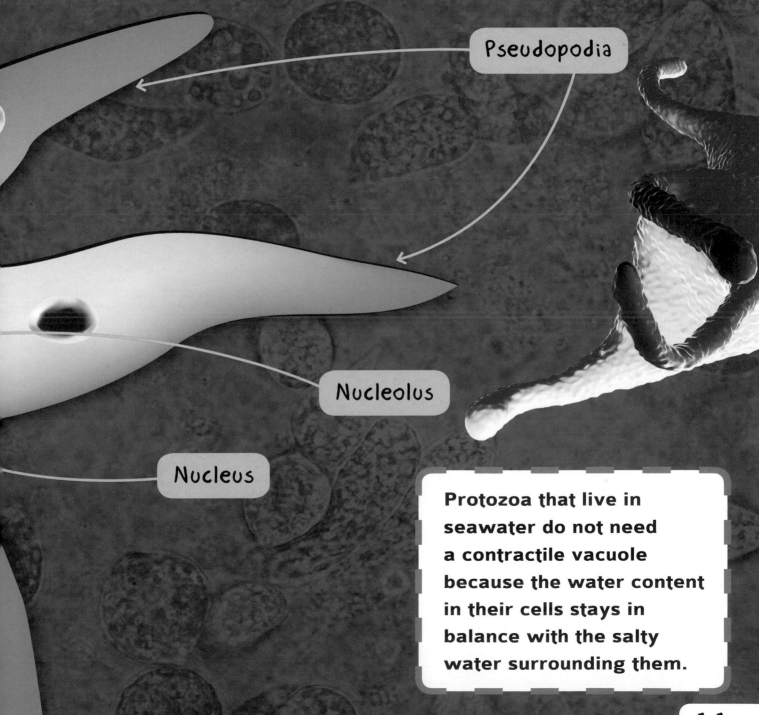

Pseudopodia

Nucleolus

Nucleus

Protozoa that live in seawater do not need a contractile vacuole because the water content in their cells stays in balance with the salty water surrounding them.

GETTING AROUND

Different species of protozoa have various ways of moving around, using different body parts. Some have structures called pseudopodia, which act like temporary feet. Cytoplasm is the fluid-like material inside cells. To move, protozoa push this cytoplasm towards one end of the cell, causing a bump in the surface. These bumps — or feet — then hold the protozoa in place while the rest of the cell catches up, moving the organism along.

"Pseudopod" comes from two Greek words, "psuedes" meaning false, and "podos" meaning foot.

Ciliates (protozoa with cilia) swim rapidly by beating the cilia in regular movements, like the oars of a boat.

Most protozoa move using permanent body parts. Some have short, hair-like structures called cilia all over the outer surface of the cell.

Some protozoa, known as flagellates, move using longer, thread-like structures called flagella. These extend from the outer surface of the cell and move through soil or water like whips. This creates waves that move the protozoa along. Some have only one flagellum, while others have several, one of which may trail behind, to help them change direction. Some protozoa, known as sporozoa, have no means of movement at all. All sporozoa are <u>parasites</u>, including *Plasmodium*, which causes the serious human disease called malaria (see page 26).

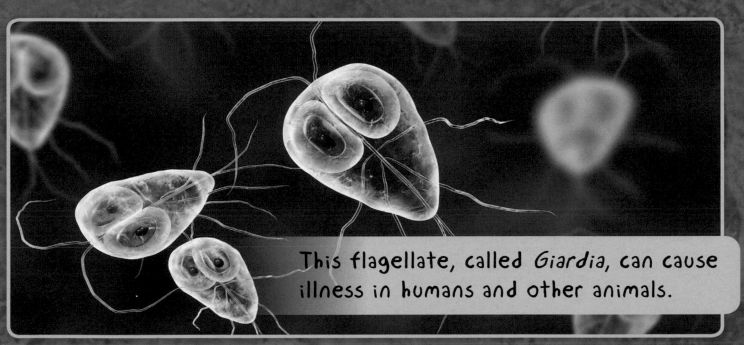

This flagellate, called *Giardia*, can cause illness in humans and other animals.

The membrane covering a protozoan cell (see page 8) also covers the pseudopodia, cilia, and flagella.

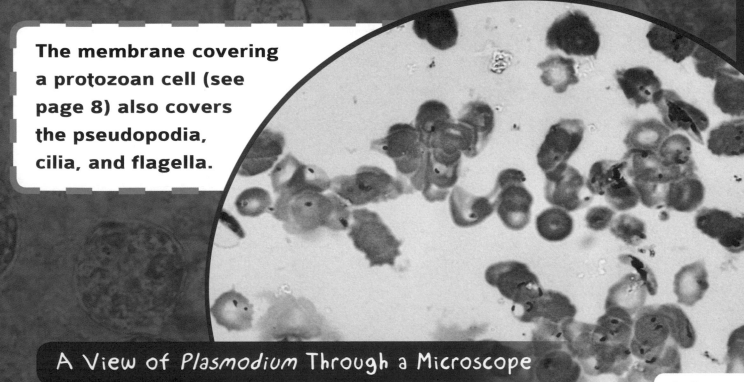

A View of *Plasmodium* Through a Microscope

13

PREDATORS AND PREY

All animals can be sorted into groups depending on what they eat. The three groups are carnivores, herbivores, and omnivores.

Some animals are also classed as detritivores, feeding on dead plant and animal matter. Different species of protozoa can be found in each of these groups.

Herbivores
Plant Eaters

Carnivores
Meat Eaters

Omnivores
Plant and Meat Eaters

Animals that hunt other animals are called predators, whereas animals that are hunted by other animals are called prey.

Although most protozoa are heterotrophs (see page 7), some, called autotrophs (say: aw-toe-troffs), make their own food by converting sunlight into sugars, just as plants do. They are at the start of the food chain because they are producers of food for other organisms along the chain.

Euglena protozoa are autotrophs but, if no sunlight is available, they can also feed on other organisms.

Most protozoa are consumers. This means they eat other organisms, such as bacteria, other protozoa, and <u>fungi</u>. In turn, protozoa are eaten by insects, fish, flat worms, water fleas, and crustaceans, such as tiny shrimp. The ability to move around helps many protozoa to find and capture prey. The cilia around the membrane of some protozoa, such as the paramecium, help to guide food into the digestive tract (gut). Some use their pseudopodia to engulf prey, which they then digest using <u>enzymes</u>.

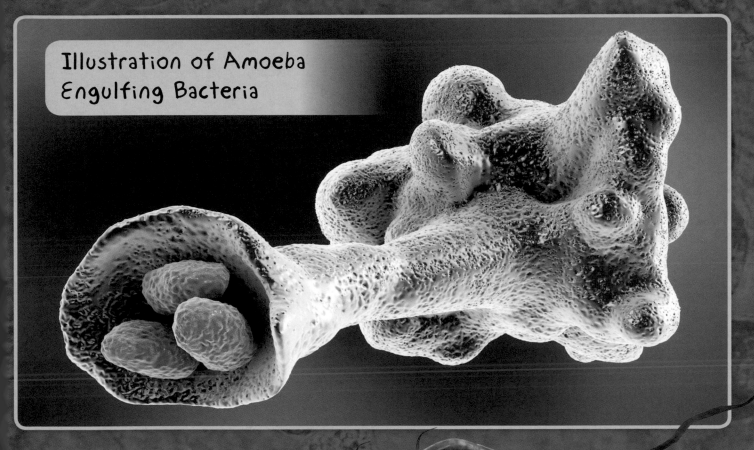

Illustration of Amoeba Engulfing Bacteria

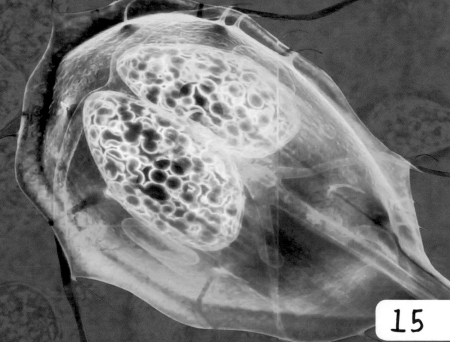

Amoebas are part of the rhizopod subphylum. With around 18,000 known species, it is the largest subphylum of protozoa.

NATURAL
HABITATS

Protozoa are found in both saltwater and freshwater habitats, including seas, rivers, estuaries, swamps, lakes, and ponds. They even live in <u>stagnant</u> water and <u>sewage</u> treatment plants! Some live in soil or in rotting plant or animal matter. Protozoa are found all over the world, even in the sea ice and freezing temperatures of Antarctica. Some protozoa are free-living, which means they can survive independently. Others live in large groups or colonies. Some protozoa are benthic – they live in sediment in a sea, lake, or riverbed.

Protozoa are found from the Antarctic in the south to the Arctic in the north, where they form a large part of the <u>plankton</u> in the sea.

A View of Plankton Through a Microscope

Some protozoa are parasites, living in or on the bodies of other creatures, including humans. These parasitic protozoa feed on the nutrients of their <u>host</u>. Sometimes, parasitic protozoa cause illness or even death to the host, but some are symbionts (say: sim-bee-onts). This means that both the protozoa and the host benefit from living together. Termites, for example, feed on dead wood but rely on protozoa that live in their gut to help them digest it. The termites would die without the protozoa and the protozoa would die outside the termites' bodies.

Toxoplasma is a protozoan parasite that lives in rats, cats, and even humans.

This termite is feeding on dead wood.

ADAPTATION

As we have seen, protozoa exist in many different forms and in every kind of habitat. This success is partly due to their ability to become <u>cysts</u>. In unsuitable conditions, amoebas, for example, can lose most of their water and then create a thick, tough wall around themselves. As cysts, they can then survive a lack of food, extreme heat or cold, or other difficult conditions. When the environment becomes suitable once more, the walls break open and the amoebas emerge.

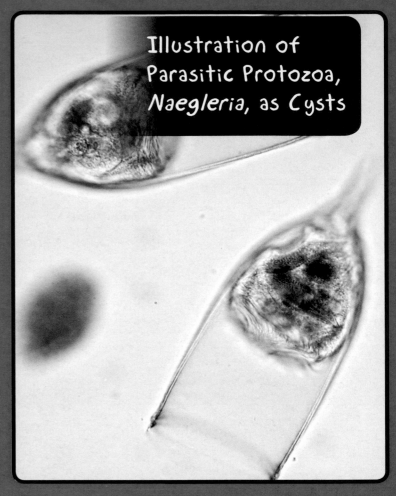

Illustration of Parasitic Protozoa, *Naegleria*, as Cysts

A View of Tintinnids Through a Microscope

Tintinnids are marine protozoa that are programmed to break out of their cysts at times of year when food is plentiful.

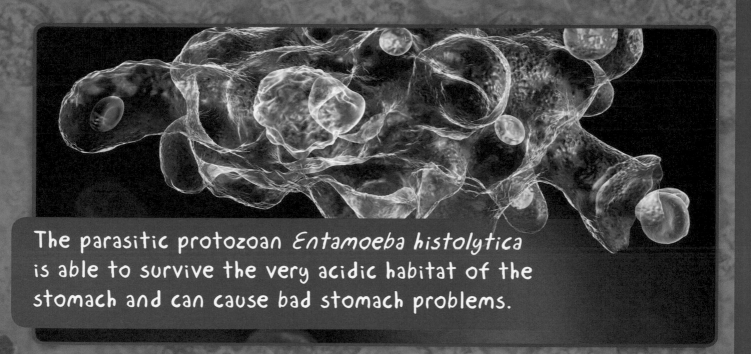

The parasitic protozoan *Entamoeba histolytica* is able to survive the very acidic habitat of the stomach and can cause bad stomach problems.

Protozoa that live in soils that freeze and thaw are able to encyst (turn into cysts) very quickly in freezing temperatures. If the soil thaws, they quickly emerge from the cysts, feed, reproduce, and then encyst again when the soil refreezes. Some freshwater protozoa, such as *Loxodes*, which live at the bottom of lakes and rivers, have different ways of adapting to difficult conditions. If oxygen levels in the water fall, they are able to swim upward to a level where oxygen is available but where they are not in competition for food with plankton.

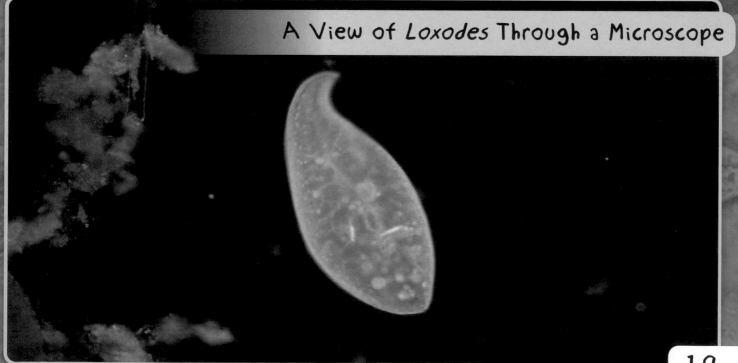

A View of *Loxodes* Through a Microscope

LIFE CYCLES

The life cycle of a plant or animal is the series of changes that it goes through from the start to the end of its life, including reproduction.

REPRODUCTION OF AMOEBAS

BINARY FISSION

Amoeba pulls in its pseudopodia.

Nucleus

Pseudopodia

Daughter nuclei create a dumbbell shape.

Nucleus divides into two daughter nuclei.

Cell splits into two daughter cells.

Different protozoa have various ways of reproducing. In the simplest form of reproduction, the cell splits into two in a process called binary fission. The nucleus splits into two parts that move to opposite ends of the cell. The cell takes on a dumbbell (figure eight) shape and then splits into two identical daughter cells. Multiple fission is a different type of cell division that takes place in the cysts of some protozoa. The original cell divides many times inside the cyst. Many daughter cells are released when the cyst wall breaks.

Nucleus

Pseudopodia

MULTIPLE FISSION

Amoeba pulls in its pseudopodia and forms a protective cyst wall.

Cyst wall breaks.

Cell divides many times inside the cyst wall.

Many daughter cells are released.

21

Although reproduction usually only requires one individual, some species of protozoa are able to reproduce in another way as well. This involves the joining together of the nuclei from two different cells. The new daughter cells contain material from both parent cells.

This material, called genetic material, gives instructions on how development takes place. The two parent cells may join together at the oral groove, a dip in the membrane that is open to the outside.

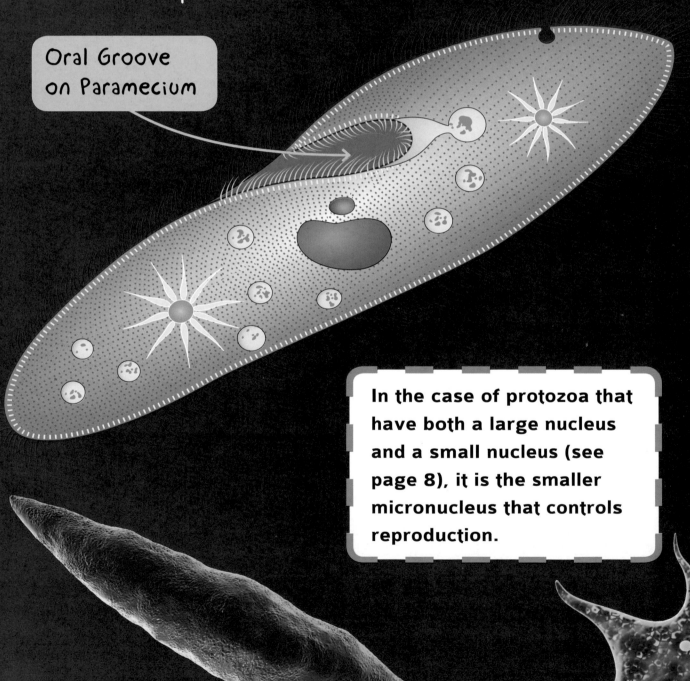

Oral Groove on Paramecium

In the case of protozoa that have both a large nucleus and a small nucleus (see page 8), it is the smaller micronucleus that controls reproduction.

LIFE CYCLE OF *ENTAMOEBA HISTOLYTICA*

Infection-causing cysts enter the human body from <u>contaminated</u> food or water.

Cyst walls break down in the small intestine. This is called excystment.

In <u>less economically developed countries</u> (LEDCs), water supplies and food can easily be contaminated by this feces. *Entamoeba histolytica* causes severe diarrhea and liver problems. The cysts can survive for weeks outside the human host before being taken in again, restarting the cycle.

Reproduction takes place in the colon. Trophozoites are produced and colonize the colon. ("Trophozoite" is a general word for the active feeding and multiplying stage of many protozoa.)

Encystment (forming of new cysts) takes place in the colon.

Infection-causing cysts pass through the rest of the digestive system. They are carried out of the body in feces (poop).

Small Intestine

Colon

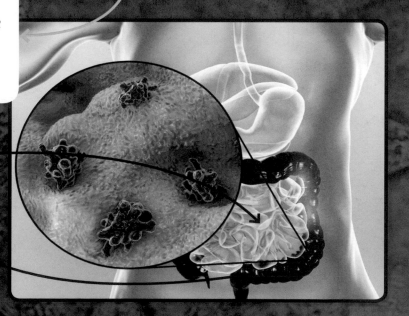

EXTREME
PROTOZOA

Some protozoa are able to survive in extremely hostile conditions. Foraminifera are marine protozoa that have a shell. They are found in oceans all over the world, in both shallow and deep waters. The deepest place on Earth is the Challenger Deep, part of the Mariana Trench in the Pacific Ocean. It is over 6.8 miles (11 km) deep, but sediment collected from it contained foraminifera. The water pressure at that depth would feel like 50 jumbo jets piled on top of you!

Foraminifera

The pressure is so high that it would <u>dissolve</u> the shells of most foraminifera, so these protozoans have a shell made out of tiny plates that are made of a clay instead.

Plate

As we have seen, despite their tiny size, protozoa can cause serious illnesses in humans. African sleeping sickness affects people in rural areas of Africa. The symptoms include fever and headaches, as well as disturbed sleep, which gives the disease its name. It is caused by a parasitic protozoan called *Trypanosoma* and is spread when people are bitten by an infected insect called the tsetse fly.

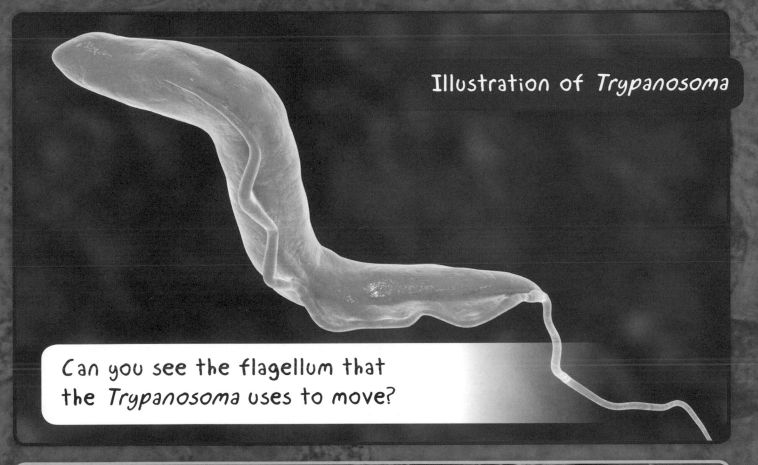

Illustration of *Trypanosoma*

Can you see the flagellum that the *Trypanosoma* uses to move?

Tsetse Fly

The Tsetse fly is a host (a carrier of the disease). The host is needed to complete the life cycle of *Trypanosoma* and pass on the disease.

MALARIA

Malaria is a life-threatening disease caused by a parasitic protozoan called *Plasmodium*. The disease is transferred from a person with malaria to a healthy person by the bite of a female *Anopheles* mosquito. The mosquito feeds on the healthy person's blood and passes on the parasites through its saliva into the bite wound. The parasites then travel to the liver of the infected person, where they multiply before entering the red blood cells. Once in the red blood cells of the bitten person, the parasites multiply again.

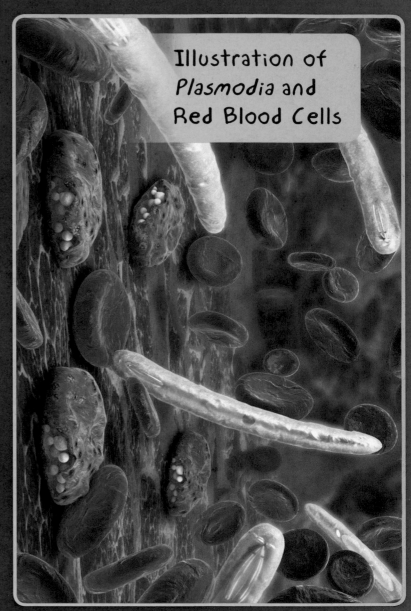

Illustration of *Plasmodia* and Red Blood Cells

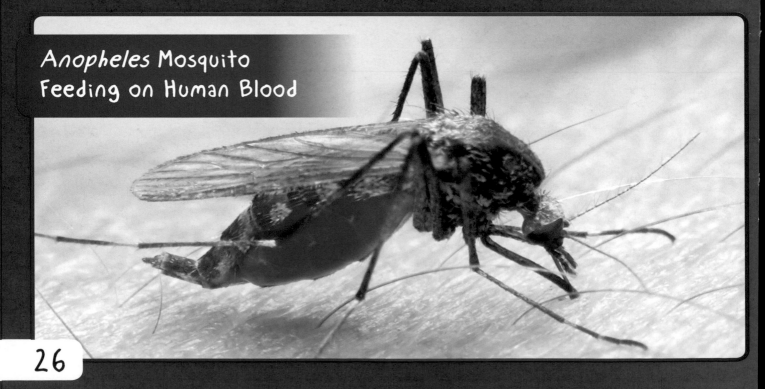

Anopheles Mosquito Feeding on Human Blood

The blood cells eventually burst, releasing infection into the blood plasma. This results in serious illness, with high fever, shaking chills, and severe flu-like symptoms. The parasites complete their development inside the mosquito, with the process beginning again as soon as a new victim is bitten. Hundreds of millions of people suffer from malaria each year worldwide and hundreds of thousands die – mostly children under age five. Drugs are available to protect people, but forms of malaria have developed that cannot be treated by even the most powerful medicines.

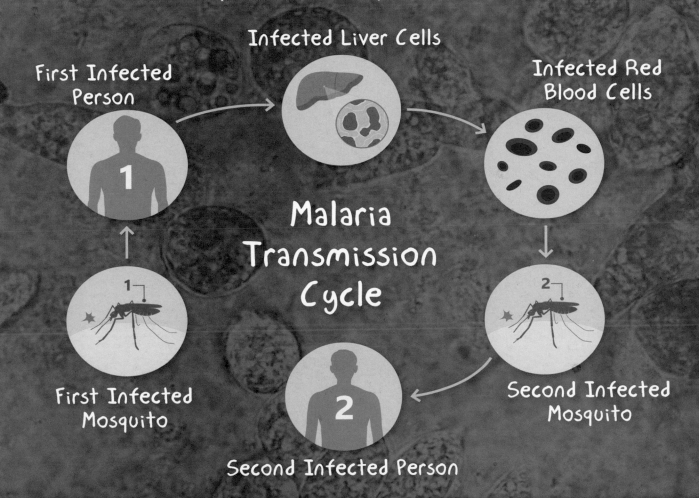

Infected Liver Cells

First Infected Person

Infected Red Blood Cells

Malaria Transmission Cycle

1

First Infected Mosquito

2

Second Infected Mosquito

Second Infected Person

Mosquitoes are most likely to bite between 9 p.m and 5 a.m, so sleeping under a net gives some protection.

PROTOZOA UNDER THREAT

Protozoa form an important part of the food chain. <u>Aquatic</u> protozoa, for example, provide food for fish and other animals. Land-based protozoa are an important food source for other soil organisms and help to make soil more fertile (able to grow strong, healthy crops). They help to control the populations of harmful bacteria and other protozoa and are therefore important in maintaining <u>biodiversity</u>. Water and land-based protozoa are also important in speeding up the rotting of dead plants and animals.

PROTOZOAN FOOD WEB

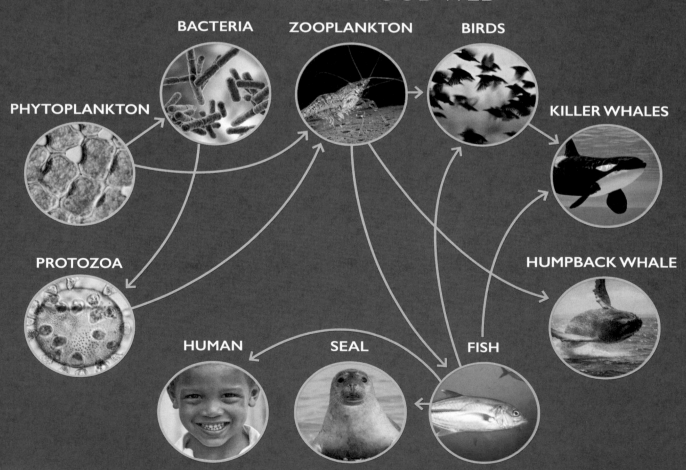

Pollution of aquatic and land-based habitats, caused by human activities, is a threat to protozoa and therefore to the food chain. Global warming is the gradual heating up of our planet, caused by burning fossil fuels (coal, oil, and gas). As they burn, they release carbon dioxide and other gases, which stop heat from escaping from the atmosphere. Carbon dioxide also dissolves into water, making it more acidic. Changes in soil and water temperatures and in water acidity affect the delicate balance of the food chain. Plastic, oil, or chemical pollution has the same effect.

This power station burns coal to produce electricity.

Marine environments all over our planet are polluted with plastic waste.

FIND OUT MORE

BOOKS

ANIMAL CLASSIFICATION
Discover and Learn by Steffi Cavell-Clarke

(Booklife 2017)

WEBSITES

BBC NATURE
www.bbc.co.uk/nature

Search under "protozoa" for information, news stories, and images.

KIDS BIOLOGY
kidsbiology.com/biology-basics/five-kingdoms/

Use this site to find out more information about how plants and animals are classified. There is a separate tab for the protozoa kingdom.

SCIENCE PHOTO
https://www.sciencephoto.com/category/animals/protozoa/all%20protozoa

Take a look at this website for some interesting images of protozoa.

GLOSSARY

adapted	changed over time to suit an environment
aquatic	living or growing near or in water
biodiversity	the variety of living things in a particular habitat
carbon dioxide	a natural, colorless gas found in air
contaminated	made unclean by adding a poisonous or polluting substance to it
crustaceans	a mainly aquatic group of animals that includes crabs, lobsters, and barnacles
cysts	tough, protective capsules that enclose the inactive stages of an organism
dissolve	become part of a liquid to form a solution
enzymes	substances produced by living organisms that help to bring about particular processes, such as digesting food
food chain	a chain in which living things rely on the previous organism in the chain for food
fungi	simple living organisms that are neither plants nor animals
host	an animal or plant in or on which a parasite lives
less economically developed countries (LEDCs)	countries where people may have lower incomes and have less access to clean water and health care
microscope	a scientific instrument that makes tiny things look many times bigger so that we can see them
molecules	the smallest units of a substance
oxygen	a natural, colorless gas found in air that living things need in order to survive
parasites	organisms that live in or on the bodies of other organisms and take their food from these other organisms
phylum	a term used to group together living things that share the same characteristics
plankton	small and microscopic organisms that drift or float in the sea or freshwater habitats
plasma	the colorless, fluid part of blood
pollution	the act of introducing to the environment a substance that is poisonous or harmful
sewage	waste water and feces
species	a group of very similar organisms that are capable of producing young together
stagnant	a term to describe water that does not flow and which usually has an unpleasant smell
transparent	a material that lets light pass through it, causing it to be see-through
unique	unlike anything else

31

INDEX